DATE DUE

JAN 3 1 1996	JAN 2 1 2003
FEB 2 0 1996	FEB 2 3 2003
MAY 2 6 1996	MAR 3 2003
NOV 3 0 1996	JUL 1 3 2003
DEC 1 4 1996	
DEC 2 8 1996	MAY 0 7 2004
MAR 0 3 1997	AUG 1 1 2004
FEB 1 1 1998	DEC 0 2 2004
OCT 2 5 1998	JAN 2 9 2005
2 6 1998	JUL 0 5 2005
JAN 3 1 1999	JUL 2 6 2005
FEB 1 5 1999	JUL 1 7 2007
MAR 2 9 1999	NOV 3 0 2007
8/9/99	MY 2 3 '08
MAR 1 7 2000	
DEC 5 2002	

DEMCO, INC. 38-2931

REVOLUTION!

THE AMERICAN REVOLUTION

R. G. Grant

Thomson Learning
New York

REVOLUTION!

The American Revolution
The Easter Rising
1848: Year of Revolution
The French Revolution

Cover picture: *Washington crossing the Delaware River before the Battle of Trenton.*
Title page: *A group of minutemen on the march.*
Contents page: *The Declaration of Independence, which was written to create the United States as an independent country.*

First published in the United States in 1995 by
Thomson Learning
New York, NY

Published simultaneously in Great Britain by Wayland (Publishers) Ltd.

Library of Congress Cataloging-in-Publication Data
Grant, R.G.
The American revolution / R.G. Grant.
　　　p.　　cm.—(Revolution! (Thomson Learning (Firm)))
　Includes bibliographical references and index.
　ISBN 1-56847-393-1 (hc)
　1. United States—History—Revolution, 1775–1783—
Juvenile literature. [1. United States—History—Revolution,
1775–1783.] I. Title. II. Series.
E208.G73　　1995
973.3—dc20　　　　　　　95-13876

Printed in Italy

Picture Acknowledgments
The publishers would like to thank the following for permission to use their pictures in this book (t = top, b = bottom, l = left, r = right): AKG London Front cover 12 (t), 29 (b), 42 (t); Robert Harding Picture Library 14–15, 41 (b); Peter Newark's American Pictures Title page 4 (b), 14 (l), 18 (b), 22 (b), 24, 28 (b), 30–31, 40–41 (t), 44 (b); Photri Inc. 4 (t), 6, 7 (t), 7 (b), 9, 11 (t), 13, 16, 18–19 (t), 19 (b), 20 (b), 20-21 (t), 22–23 (t), 25, 26, 26–27, 32, 33, 34 (t), 35, 36 (t), 36 (b), 37, 38, 39, 42–43 (b), 44 (t); Range Pictures/The Bettmann Archive contents page, 11 (b), 12 (b), 21 (r), 28–29 (t), 34 (b); Range/ Bettmann/Hulton 8; ZEFA 23 (b). Maps by Peter Bull.

CONTENTS

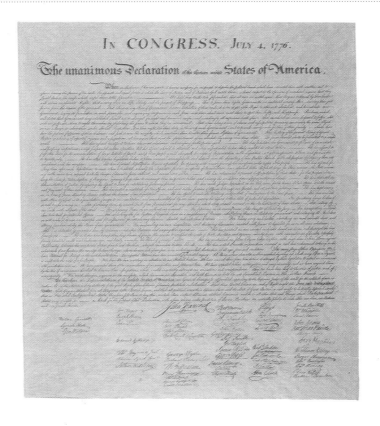

THE SEEDS OF REVOLUTION

In Boston, Massachusetts, the evening of March 5, 1770 was crisp and cold. Snow lay in the cobbled streets. The mood in the town, one of the largest ports in Great Britain's North American empire, was tense and ugly. Eighteen months earlier British soldiers had been sent to defend customs officials from attacks by angry townspeople. As agents of British power, the "redcoats" were not welcome in the town because the Bostonians were refusing to pay customs duties imposed by the British.

On March 5, there were scattered fights throughout the day between locals and British troops. In the evening, the rumor spread that British soldiers had beaten up two Boston youths, aged 11 and 14. Fire bells rang out across the moonlit town and an angry crowd gathered. A small contingent of British troops under the command of Captain Thomas Preston was on duty outside the Customs House in King Street. They confronted a defiant, furious mass of the Boston poor, apprentices and artisans waving wooden clubs, shouting insults, and pelting the soldiers with snowballs.

Right: *This engraving of the Boston Massacre was made by American rebel Paul Revere. It was anti-British propaganda and is not an accurate picture of what happened on March 5, 1770.*

"Fire, damn you! Fire!" someone called from the crowd. A stick was thrown and struck a soldier, Private Hugh Montgomery, and knocked him to the ground. Montgomery panicked. He clambered to his feet and fired into the crowd, calling on his comrades to do the same. Before Captain Preston could regain control of his men, they had fired point-blank into the mass of civilians. In half a minute the street was empty. Only the dead and the wounded were left on the ground. Three Americans had been killed outright—among them Crispus Attucks, a runaway slave—and two others later died of their wounds.

Left: British soldiers arrest an American farmer and drive his family off their land. By the 1770s, many Americans saw the British—especially the British army—as a threat to their freedom.

AMERICAN SOCIETY

The American Revolution took place in 13 British colonies between Canada in the north and Florida in the south (see page 10). The population of the 13 colonies in 1775 was about 2.5 million. Although small, this population was increasing very fast. In 1700 it had been only 275,000; by 1800 it would be 5.3 million.

Large landowners, rich merchants, and lawyers, all white, made up an elite in all the colonies. They copied the fashions of English gentlemen, passing their time at cards and billiards in their large fashionable houses. Their strong sense of their rights led them to expect to run their own affairs without interference from Great Britain. Reluctantly, these gentlemen became revolutionaries.

The majority of white Americans were small farmers, artisans, or shopkeepers. Neither rich nor poor, they were people with a strong sense of independence who thought for themselves, and almost all of them could read and write. These people were the backbone of the revolution.

The poorest whites were landless farmhands and unskilled laborers in the towns. For many such people, the 1760s and 1770s were hard times. The economy was depressed, wages were low, and there was not enough work for everyone. Hardship often made poor people angry and ready to join riots against British soldiers, customs officials, and wealthy pro-British Americans.

At the bottom of colonial society were the African Americans. They numbered around half a million, about one in five of the population, and almost all were slaves. They had virtually no rights and could be bought and sold as personal property.

There were also about 200,000 Native Americans living in and around the 13 colonies. They lived in their own nations with their own leaders.

Indignant Bostonians armed themselves and called for support from neighboring towns to fight the soldiers. But the authorities stopped the bloodshed by promising to arrest those responsible for the Boston Massacre. When the soldiers came to trial, they were defended by American lawyers, including John Adams, a future president. Adams, in common with other Americans, disapproved of mob violence. He described the Boston crowd contemptuously as "a motley rabble of saucy boys." A jury found Captain Preston innocent. Two soldiers were convicted of manslaughter, not murder. Their sole punishment was to be branded on the thumb with the letter M. But, most importantly, the British army withdrew from Boston.

Resisting British Power

Radical patriots, like John Adams's cousin Sam Adams and the Boston silversmith Paul Revere, had directed the campaign to force the soldiers out. The radicals were also known as the Sons of Liberty. Since the 1760s, they had led opposition to every British attempt to tax the North American colonies. They resisted the Stamp Act in 1765 and forced the British to abandon it. They opposed the Townshend Acts in 1767, which imposed new import duties to be collected by British-appointed customs officials. In 1770 the British once more backed down, withdrawing the duties on all items except tea,

Left: *Paul Revere was a Boston silversmith and printer. He is most famous for his dramatic night ride to warn of a British attack (see page 15).*

(see page 15).

TIME LINE

1763
February 10: The Peace of Paris ends the French and Indian War; Great Britain gains possession of Quebec and the Floridas.
1765
March 22: Great Britain introduces the Stamp Act.
1767
June 29: The Townshend Acts impose duties on many items imported into the North American colonies, including tea.
1770
March 5: The Boston Massacre—five people killed by British soldiers.
1773
December 16: The Boston Tea Party—rebels dump East India tea into the ocean.
1774
March-June: Great Britain imposes the Intolerable Acts and appoints General Thomas Gage as military governor of Massachusetts.
September 5: The First Continental Congress meets in Philadelphia.

SMUGGLING

A major cause of disagreement between Great Britain and its colonies was Great Britain's attempt to control American trade to its own advantage. Great Britain imposed a host of rules and regulations known as the Navigation Acts. Many Americans refused to respect these rules and became involved in smuggling, which could be highly lucrative. It was, for example, the source of the rebel leader John Hancock's fortune.

Popular opinion in the colonies did not see smuggling as wrong. In 1772 the British Royal Navy's schooner *Gaspee* ran aground near Providence, Rhode Island, while searching for smugglers. The delighted Rhode Islanders set the helpless vessel on fire and, although everyone in the community knew who had taken part in this attack, not a single individual could be found to testify against the attackers.

Left: *In 1775 American patriots, called the Sons of Liberty, organized protests like this against the Stamp Act, which they described as "England's folly and America's ruin."*

Above: *John Hancock was a Boston merchant. His family's wealth came from trade that was illegal under British laws. Hancock became one of the leaders of the revolution.*

then a popular beverage in the American colonies.

The tactics used to resist unpopular British taxes were often rough. American patriots tarred and feathered unpopular officials, attacked customs houses, and ransacked the mansions of pro-British American "Tories." Most wealthier Americans disliked and feared such mob tactics, but they joined in organized boycotts of British goods. Feeling against Great Britain was running high. John Wentworth, the governor of New Hampshire, wrote that "a dangerous spirit is rooting in the minds of the people, who begin to think Britain intends to enslave and destroy them...." [1]

The Boston Tea Party

In 1773 the smoldering conflict between England and the colonies suddenly flared up into an uncontrollable blaze. The spark was the British decision to allow the East India Company to sell tea directly to the American colonies instead of auctioning it to middlemen. The price of tea in the colonies would fall dramatically, but the threepenny import duty on tea imposed by the Townshend Acts remained. The Sons of Liberty rejected the idea of paying import duties imposed by the British Parliament.

As the first ships carrying East India tea arrived in American ports, they met with resistance everywhere. It was in Boston that events came to a head. In November, three tea-laden ships, the *Dartmouth*, *Eleanor*, and *Beaver*, arrived in Boston Harbor. Local people, urged on by radicals such as Sam Adams and John Hancock, stopped the tea from being unloaded. But the governor of Massachusetts, Thomas Hutchinson, a wealthy Bostonian, refused to let the ships leave port without unloading their cargo. Hutchinson hated and feared what he saw as "mob rule" in Boston. He had decided it was time for the authorities to take a stand.

SAM ADAMS (1722–1803)

Harvard-educated Samuel Adams, a former tax collector, was one of the principal Sons of Liberty who organized resistance to British rule. He was a natural rebel. "If I am to have a master," he wrote, "let me have a severe one. I shall be constantly disposed to taking the first fair opportunity of ridding myself of his tyranny."[2] Adams believed the British were plotting to reduce all Americans to slavery, and he played a leading part in building up resistance to their rule. He enjoyed a distinguished political career during the revolution and after.

Above: *A leader of the Sons of Liberty, Samuel Adams dedicated his life to resisting British rule. In 1773 he led opposition to the import tax on tea.*

Above: *Boston citizens cheer as patriots disguised as Native Americans throw chests of tea into the sea. The Boston Tea Party convinced the British government that strict measures were needed to make Bostonians obey the law.*

On December 16 a mass meeting was held at Boston's Old South Meeting House. Chaired by Sam Adams, the meeting called for the three tea-laden ships to leave immediately. The commander of the ships asked Governor Hutchinson for permission to do this, but his request was refused. Shortly after 6 p.m., Adams banged his gavel three times and declared: "This meeting can do nothing more to save the country." It was the signal for direct action. With no British soldiers to stop them, about one thousand people ran down to where the ships were anchored. They were led by a group disguised as Native Americans armed with axes. Clambering aboard, they split open the tea chests and hurled their contents into the water, cheered on by a large crowd of onlookers.

THE THIRTEEN COLONIES

Before the outbreak of the revolution, there were few links among the 13 British colonies. Neighboring colonies were often hostile to one another, quarreling over territory and trade.

Most were royal colonies. These were officially ruled by a governor appointed by Great Britain. Only Rhode Island and Connecticut elected their own governors. Pennsylvania, Maryland, and Delaware were proprietary colonies, where authority was held by a single family—the Penns in Pennsylvania and Delaware and the Calverts in Maryland.

In practice, all the colonies were used to running their own affairs through an elected assembly. The vote was limited to white male property owners—the poor, women, and Native and African Americans were excluded. Wealthy landowners, merchants, and lawyers dominated the elected assemblies, but the colonies were still much more democratic than England or any other major European country at the time.

To the north of the 13 colonies, Great Britain controlled Quebec and Nova Scotia. These Canadian colonies did not join in the American Revolution and neither did the British-owned Floridas to the south.

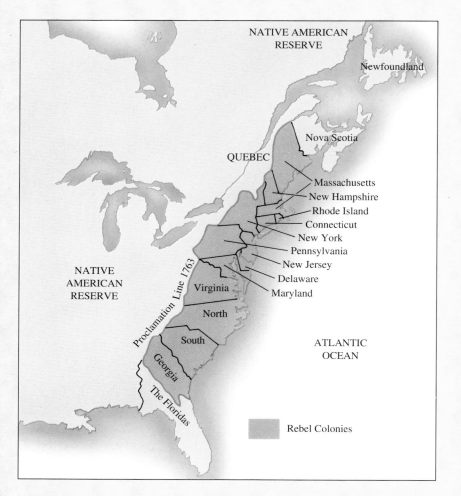

Left: *This map shows how North America was divided among different British colonies before the American Revolution. The largest single colony in terms of wealth and population was Virginia. The British had reserved all the land west of the Appalachian Mountains for Native Americans.*

The Intolerable Acts

The Boston Tea Party, as it came to be known, was a symbolic act in defiance of Great Britain. The British decided that the lawless people of Massachusetts had to be taught a lesson. In 1774 the British Parliament passed four measures, known in America as the Intolerable Acts. The most oppressive of these acts closed Boston Harbor until the tea was paid for. British army commander General Thomas Gage was made governor of Massachusetts and put the colony under military rule. The redcoats marched back into Boston.

The British hoped that Massachusetts might be isolated, but all the colonies rallied to its support. A South Carolina politician, David Ramsay, spoke for most Americans when he denounced the Intolerable Acts as "a complete system of tyranny." The other colonies could see that what happened to Massachusetts might happen to them. In September 1774 all the colonies except Georgia sent representatives to the First Continental Congress held in Philadelphia. Congress agreed to set up a continental association to organize a boycott of British imports. It boldly asserted that only the elected colonial assemblies had the right to pass laws for Americans and to tax them. The Congress called for resistance to the Intolerable Acts.

Above: *Prayers are said at the opening of the First Continental Congress gathered in Carpenters' Hall, Philadelphia. The Congress agreed to organize a boycott of British trade. Delegates called on the British government to recognize Americans' natural right to "life, liberty, and property."*

Left: *General Thomas Gage, the British military governor of Massachusetts, is visited by Boston children pleading for fairer treatment of their town. The black servant who is tending the fire is almost certainly a slave.*

In New England, American patriots took the law into their own hands. Tea drinkers were assaulted, and many people took a public pledge never to drink tea again. Tax collectors and other officials were tarred and feathered. Some prominent pro-British Americans, including Governor Thomas Hutchinson, fled to Great Britain in fear of their lives.

The people of Massachusetts defied General Gage's military government. The Massachusetts legislature, dissolved by Gage, met on its own authority as a provincial congress and effectively took control of Massachusetts. The Massachusetts Committee of Public Safety was set up, headed by John Hancock. It urged communities to train local militias to resist British rule. The British also prepared for conflict. In November 1774 King George III declared that "blows must decide whether they are to be subject to this country or independent." [3] The stage was set for war.

Above: *George III was king of Great Britain for 60 years, from 1760 to 1820. At the time of the American Revolution he was a young and active ruler, but later in life he suffered from blindness and periods of insanity.*

Left: *This cartoon shows violent American resistance to British officials. A tax collector has been tarred and feathered, and he is being forced to drink the hated British tea.*

Right: *Patrick Henry delivers his famous speech in Williamsburg, Virginia. Henry later was governor of Virginia, during and after the revolution.*

WHY THE COLONIES REBELLED

Relations between Great Britain and the 13 colonies began to worsen after the end of the French and Indian War in 1763, which drove France out of North America. Until then, Great Britain had paid little attention to its colonies. But now it decided to keep an army permanently stationed in North America and wanted the colonies to pay for it. Most Americans resented the army's presence, and no one wished to pay the cost of its upkeep.

When the British Parliament tried to impose taxes on the colonies, the Americans rejected what they called "taxation without representation." The Americans believed that people should only pay taxes approved by an assembly that they had elected. Since American citizens had not elected the British Parliament it could not tax them. Massachusetts lawyer James Otis said, "Taxation without representation is tyranny."

The British then tried to evade American objections to taxation by using customs duties instead of taxes to raise revenue. They argued that duties were an external tax and that everyone accepted Great Britain's right to control its colonies' trade. But the American colonies also rejected this, claiming that the British could only impose customs duties with the consent of the colonial assemblies.

The British government wanted more control over the American colonies. They saw themselves as upholding law and order against rebellious radicals. But many Americans believed that the British themselves were breaking the spirit of the law. They thought that the British were bent on destroying traditional freedoms, especially after the Intolerable Acts of 1774. The Americans felt justified in resisting this tyranny, by force if necessary.

LIBERTY OR DEATH

The finest expression of American defiance of British rule was lawyer Patrick Henry's address to the House of Burgesses, in Virginia, on March 23, 1775. A rousing call to action, the speech ended: "Why stand we here idle?...Is life so dear, or peace so sweet, as to be purchased at the price of chains and slavery? Forbid it, Almighty God! I know not what course others may take, but as for me, give me liberty, or give me death!"

"THE SHOT HEARD AROUND THE WORLD"

The British military governor in Massachusetts, General Thomas Gage, was not optimistic about his situation early in 1775. His political masters 3,000 miles away in Great Britain confidently urged him to put down the rebels. They believed that the rebellion was the work of a small minority of lawless radicals. But Gage knew that most people in Massachusetts supported the rebellion. John Hancock's Committee of Public Safety was organizing militias in every town and village. Farmers and shopkeepers brought out their hunting guns and practiced drills on the local common. These armed civilians were called minutemen, because they swore to be ready to fight at a minute's notice. General Gage's redcoats only controlled Boston. The rest of Massachusetts was hostile territory.

Above: *A group of American minutemen on the march. The minutemen were mostly farmers and shopkeepers, but their courage made up for lack of military experience.*

Left: *Paul Revere rides through the night to warn the people of Lexington that British soldiers are on their way. Although Revere's midnight ride is the most famous, there were two other riders that night, Samuel Prescott and William Dawes.*

TIME LINE

1775
April 19: Massachusetts militiamen clash with the British army at Lexington and Concord.
May 10: Fort Ticonderoga falls to rebels led by Ethan Allen and Benedict Arnold.
June 15: The Continental Army is formed under the command of George Washington.
June 17: The British defeat the Americans at the Battle of Bunker Hill, but at the cost of many lives.
1776
January 10: Thomas Paine's *Common Sense* is published, calling for independence and a republican government.
March 17: The British army abandons Boston.
June: The last American rebels are driven out of Canada.
July 4: Congress approves the Declaration of Independence.

On the night of April 18–19, 1775, 16 handpicked companies of British soldiers left Boston on a secret mission into rebel country. They intended to raid the town of Concord, 15 miles away, and destroy a large store of rebel weapons. They also had orders to arrest Sam Adams and John Hancock. But the secret of the attack was known to local patriots. As the soldiers set out, so did three American messengers, including Paul Revere. Riding at breakneck speed along moonlit roads patrolled by British soldiers, they succeeded in alerting the local minutemen. Paul Revere was eventually captured by the British and was lucky to escape with his life.

The main British force reached the village of Lexington at dawn. They were met by 70 local militiamen, commanded by Captain John Parker, lined up on the village common. Hopelessly outnumbered, the Americans decided to disperse. Suddenly a shot rang out. No one knew who had fired, but the British soldiers immediately unleashed a volley of shots. After a brief one-sided battle, eight Americans lay dead.

The British moved on to Concord and, at the town's North Bridge, fighting began in earnest. Spurred on by anger at the invasion of their town, several hundred militiamen drove their attackers back. The British officers were forced to order a retreat. The poet Ralph Waldo Emerson later described the first shot at North Bridge as "The shot heard around the world." It was the true start of the War of Independence.

Stumbling back exhausted from Concord to Boston, the redcoats were mercilessly harassed by hidden snipers along the roadside. A British soldier, Ensign Jeremy Lister, wrote that there was "a general firing on us from all quarters, from behind hedges and walls."[4] Men swarmed from the surrounding farms to take a shot at the British. Lieutenant John Barker described how the rebels' numbers increased "while ours were reducing by deaths, wounds, and fatigue, and we were totally surrounded with such an incessant fire as it is impossible to conceive."[5] Seventy-three British soldiers died and around two hundred were wounded or missing. They had suffered a humiliating defeat.

Below: *The British army marches into Concord on April 19, 1775. Armed resistance from the American rebels came as a severe shock to the British commanders.*

The Battle of Bunker Hill

Once the British soldiers were back in Boston, the rebel militiamen fortified roads and hills around the edge of the town. The only way in or out of Boston for the British was now by sea. During May 1775 troop reinforcements arrived from Great Britain along with three more generals, William Howe, John Burgoyne, and Henry Clinton. They persuaded Gage that he needed to take control of the hills on the nearby Charlestown peninsula before the rebels set up guns there to bombard Boston. But once again the rebels discovered Gage's plans. On June 16 they took a defensive position on Bunker Hill and Breed's Hill before the British could make their move.

Below: *This map shows the position of American and British troops that led to the Battle of Bunker Hill, one of the bloodiest battles of the revolution.*

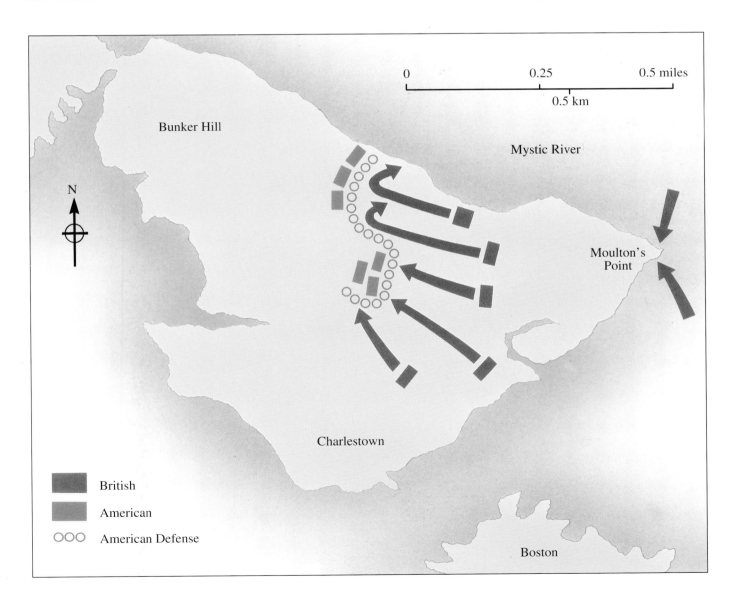

The following day Gage launched an attack on Breed's Hill. Spectators crowded the high points of Boston to get a good view. General Burgoyne described it as "one of the greatest scenes of war that can be conceived." British warships were bombarding the American positions and Charlestown was on fire. In their bright scarlet coats, the British soldiers advanced in line abreast up the hill. Dug into trenches, the unbloodied militiamen waited.

The American militiamen were ordered not to fire "until you can see the whites of their eyes." When they did let off their first volley, it shattered the advancing British forces. Time and again the British resumed their advance, only to falter once more under the withering fire. When the Americans were almost out of ammunition, the British broke through their lines. The redcoats set to work with their bayonets, stabbing the fleeing militiamen. In the scramble to escape from Breed's Hill and Bunker Hill, over four hundred Americans were wounded or killed. But the British had suffered more than one thousand casualties and, although they claimed a victory, it was a hollow one.

PATRIOTS DRIVE OUT A GOVERNOR

In July 1775, the house of the New Hampshire governor, John Wentworth, was surrounded by American patriots. His wife Frances described how the patriots forced the governor and his family to flee: "They stove at the house with clubs, brought a large cannon and placed it before the door and swore to fire through the house. They were so cruel as to affirm no one person, man, woman or child, should escape with life…. We quit the house with great haste. It was sundown and damp air. We got into the boat with our poor child…and hurried away. We had not time to get a hat or blanket for him but thought ourselves fortunate to get him off alive…. They were so cruel as to say if they could get the governor's fat child they would split him down the back and broil him." [6]

Above: *A rich American supporter of the British is thrown out of town by the patriots. They have tied him up and are carrying him through the streets for everyone to see.*

Left: *British General John Burgoyne was known as "Gentleman Johnny" because of his taste for good living. His military career ended in disgrace at Saratoga, but he was later successful as a writer of comedies.*

Right: *The Battle of Bunker Hill, seen from the deck of a British warship. As the redcoats attack the American positions, the village of Charlestown is set on fire by shells from the British ship's guns.*

National Uprising

As the war started in Massachusetts, British power was collapsing throughout the 13 colonies. One by one, the British-appointed governors were thrown out and provincial congresses took control of government. The Earl of Dunmore, governor of Virginia, declared martial law and tried to rally loyalist forces. But even he had to take refuge on a British frigate when people rioted in the streets of the Virginia capital of Williamsburg. In some areas pro-British Americans fought back.

On May 10, 1775 the Second Continental Congress met in Philadelphia. Among its members were Thomas Jefferson, Benjamin Franklin, John and Sam Adams, John Hancock, and Richard Henry Lee. The Congress agreed to set up a permanent Continental Army. It would be a stronger force than the part-time militias and include men from all 13 colonies. This army was put under the command of a 43-year-old Virginia landowner, General George Washington.

THOMAS JEFFERSON (1743–1826)

Thomas Jefferson was born in 1743. Like George Washington, he was a wealthy Virginia plantation owner. He wrote the first draft of the Declaration of Independence in 1776 and became the first United States secretary of state in 1790. As president from 1801 to 1809, he dressed and behaved in a relaxed, informal way that showed his distrust of all rulers, including himself.

Above: Apart from his political activities, Thomas Jefferson was a successful amateur architect, botanist, and inventor.

Jefferson was a genuine believer in freedom, but like all Virginia landowners he owned slaves. This was a contradiction he never overcame. Jefferson died at Monticello in Virginia on the 50th anniversary of the Declaration of Independence, July 4, 1826. Strangely, fellow rebel and the second U.S. president, John Adams, died on the same day.

Above: *General George Washington takes command of the Continental Army. The army was often unruly and disorderly before Washington took charge to enforce strict military discipline.*

Right: *Women in Philadelphia sew clothes for the American soldiers. Many American women supported the revolution, but men would not allow them to take part in the fighting or in political debates.*

"REMEMBER THE LADIES"

In 1776 Abigail Adams, the wife of John Adams, urged her husband to "remember the ladies" when forming the new United States. But women did not gain any political or legal rights in the Revolution. They were not allowed to vote, and they remained under the control of their fathers or husbands.

Women made great contributions to the Revolution. Abigail Adams, like other wives throughout the United States, ran the family farm while her husband was away making politics or war. Poorer women performed essential tasks in the army as nurses or general workers. But the contributions of women to the Revolutionary War was given little value by men.

At first the Continental Army, which was camped outside Boston, was weak and ill-disciplined. As part time militiamen, the independent-minded Americans had fought like tigers, but they did not take easily to regular soldiering. Officers were not obeyed and desertion was common. Washington adopted tough measures. A chaplain, the Reverend William Emerson, soon reported: "Everyone is made to know his place and keep in it, or be tied up and receive forty or fifty lashes according to his crime."[7]

Poorly equipped and disorganized, Washington's army was very vulnerable during this period. But the British stayed on the defensive, bottled up in Boston. Meanwhile, an American force led by former New Haven shipowner Benedict Arnold, and a rebellious frontiersman from Connecticut, Ethan Allen, captured Fort Ticonderoga at the southern end of Lake Champlain. In the winter of 1775–76 the Americans advanced northward into Quebec. The local population of French settlers refused to rise up against the British, however, and the American force was driven back.

By the spring of 1776, the British army in Boston was in a miserable state. Frozen and bored, they had spent the winter in almost total inactivity. They had to pull down buildings to get wood for fires. Food stocks were running low. General Washington had an army of 17,000 men outside the town. In March the rebels set up cannons at

GEORGE WASHINGTON (1732–1799)

George Washington has often been called "the father of his country." Born in 1732, he was a wealthy Virginia plantation owner. He became a general and commanded the Continental Army throughout the Revolutionary War. After peace was signed with Great Britain in 1783, Washington retired to his estate at Mount Vernon, intending to live and die "an honest man on my own farm." In 1789 Washington reluctantly agreed to become the first president of the United States, although he refused to accept a salary. Washington died in 1799.

Right: *George Washington fought as an officer in the Virginia militia during the French and Indian War, which ended in 1763. He is seen here wearing the uniform of the Virginia militia.*

Above: *General William Howe directs the evacuation of British troops from Boston on the night of March 17, 1776. The following day Washington's army took over the town.*

SHARPSHOOTERS

In the summer of 1775, ten companies of frontiersmen arrived in Washington's camp. These wild men wore moccasins and carried tomahawks. Armed with the famous Kentucky rifle, they were, according to John Adams, "the most accurate marksmen in the world." An Englishman reported that the frontier marksmen "will hit a card nine times out of ten" at 150 yards.

Throughout the War of Independence, American marksmen took a heavy toll on British troops, especially officers. The British soldiers were armed with inaccurate muskets and mostly fought in the open. They feared and despised the American use of snipers hidden behind trees or rocks.

The American sharpshooters had a song that mocked the British attitude: "It was not fair to shoot at us from behind trees. If they had stood open as they ought before our great guns we should have beat them with ease."

Below: *Part of a poster advertising for volunteers to join the American Continental Army. It shows the drill practiced by the soldiers and the army's new uniform.*

Dorchester Heights overlooking Boston and began a bombardment. General Howe, who had taken over command from the disgraced General Gage, decided that his position in Boston was impossible. On March 17, under cover of darkness, Howe embarked his men on ships along with one thousand loyalist Americans. They sailed off to Nova Scotia. Washington's jubilant soldiers marched into Boston. For the time being, the British army had been driven out of the 13 colonies.

A DISGRACE TO THE NAME OF SOLDIER

George Washington described the soldiers of his Continental Army as "an exceedingly dirty and nasty people." A visitor to the army's encampment in 1775 confirmed the filthiness of the soldiers, writing: "The army in general is...most wretchedly clothed, and as dirty a set of mortals as ever disgraced the name of a soldier. They have no women in the camp to do washing for the men, and they in general not being used to doing things of this sort...choose rather to let their linen rot upon their backs than to be at the trouble of cleaning 'em themselves."[8]

When the men did bathe, it also caused trouble. General Washington was forced to ban bathing "near the bridge in Cambridge, where it has been observed and complained of that many men, lost to all sense of decency and common modesty, are running about, naked, upon the bridge whilst passengers, and even ladies of the first fashion in the neighbourhood, are passing over it, as if they meant to glory in their shame."[9]

The Road to Independence

Most Americans were reluctant revolutionaries. When the Second Continental Congress met in May 1775, only a small minority of the delegates wanted independence. In July the Congress sent "The Olive Branch Petition" to King George III. It declared loyalty to the monarch and a desire for reconciliation. The king's response was a proclamation calling for the use of force to suppress the "open and avowed rebellion" in the colonies.

However, the Americans did have friends in Great Britain. British radicals, such as John Wilkes and Tom Paine, supported the colonists, and the statesman Edmund Burke pleaded for an agreement to end the "American troubles," but it was in vain. The king and his prime minister, Lord North, were determined to crush the American Revolution by force.

Many Americans argued that while they rejected the rule of the British Parliament, they remained loyal to the

Below: *Led by Thomas Jefferson, the five-man committee that drew up the Declaration of Independence presents the finished document to Congress.*

king. But early in 1776 Tom Paine published a violent attack on the monarch entitled *Common Sense*. It sold 120,000 copies in three months. Perhaps more than any other single person, Paine persuaded Americans that they should continue to campaign for total independence.

In April 1776, North Carolina became the first colony to tell its congressional delegates to vote for independence. Virginia did the same in May. On June 7, Virginian delegate Richard Henry Lee proposed "that these United Colonies are, and of right ought to be, free and independent states."

During July, while the Declaration of Independence was being drawn up, the issue of independence was still hotly debated. Some colonies, including Pennsylvania and New York, only decided to support independence at the last moment. But on July 4, 1776 the Declaration was approved. On September 9, Congress authorized the United States as the official name of the new nation. A new era in human history had begun.

Above: *Richard Henry Lee, one of the Virginia delegates to Congress, was the first to formally propose that the 13 colonies should declare themselves fully independent of Great Britain.*

THE DECLARATION OF INDEPENDENCE

On June 11, 1776 Congress appointed a committee of five men—Benjamin Franklin, Thomas Jefferson, John Adams, Robert Livingston, and Roger Sherman—to prepare a Declaration of Independence. The first draft of the Declaration was written by Thomas Jefferson. The final document was approved by Congress on July 4.

The Declaration set out revolutionary political ideas. It expressed an idealistic belief in equality, human rights, and government by consent: "We hold these truths to be self-evident, that all men are created equal, that they are endowed by their Creator with certain unalienable rights, that among these are life, liberty, and the pursuit of happiness—that to secure these rights, governments are instituted among men, deriving their just powers from the consent of the governed, that whenever any form of government becomes destructive of those ends, it is the right of the people to alter or to abolish it...."

The first man to sign the Declaration of Independence was the president of congress, John Hancock. He signed with such a flourish that his name is now used as a slang term for a signature.

DEFENDING INDEPENDENCE

The Americans had started a revolution. Now they had to defend it. In early July 1776, as the Declaration of Independence was being debated in Congress, a British army of over 30,000 men under General Howe landed on Staten Island, New York, which then had a population of only 3,000. Howe's task was to achieve the reconquest of North America. At first it did not seem to be an impossible project. Many of the American troops defending Long Island and Manhattan were in battle for the first time. Faced by heavy cannons and the muskets and bayonets of professional soldiers, they fled in fear. Although Howe was unimaginative and slow, he steadily drove Washington's forces back and captured New York City in September. It was clear that the war was going to prove long and costly.

As American commander-in-chief, Washington had an unenviable task. He was constantly short of men, weapons,

"BUT ONE LIFE TO LOSE"

After the British occupied Long Island in September 1776, a 21-year-old American officer named Nathan Hale was sent behind British lines to gather information. He was captured by the British and hanged as a spy. Facing the noose, Hale reportedly said: "I only regret that I have but one life to lose for my country." [10] The bravery with which he met his end made him a hero with the American patriots. His example raised their spirits during a dark and difficult phase of the war.

Right: *Nathan Hale faces execution as a spy.*

and money to pay his troops. The soldiers were ordinary folk who longed to return to their farms or shops. Many drifted back home when they felt like it. As the war dragged on, not enough volunteers could be found, so soldiers had to be drafted. The conscripts were mostly poor, since wealthier people were able to buy their way out of military service.

Left: British soldiers take over the streets of New York in September 1776. Many New Yorkers were loyalists and welcomed the British.

AMERICANS DIVIDED

It is generally thought that about 20 percent of Americans were loyalists who supported the British cause, 40 percent were patriots who enthusiastically backed independence, and the other 40 percent were undecided.

This meant that the War of Independence was also a civil war. All kinds of people were loyalists, from laborers and farmers to wealthy merchants and landowners. Families were divided—Benjamin Franklin signed the Declaration of Independence, but his son William was the head of the Board of American Loyalists.

When the British captured Long Island, New York, in September 1776, many people welcomed them with open arms. American loyalists formed regiments such as the Royal Greens, the Caledonian Volunteers, and Butler's Rangers, who fought alongside the British. Local revolutionary militias drove loyalists from their homes and confiscated their property.

TIME LINE

1776
August 27: General Washington is defeated on Long Island and retreats to Manhattan.
September 15: The British capture the town of New York and invade New Jersey.
December 26: General Washington defeats the British under General Howe at Trenton.
1777
September 26: British forces occupy Philadelphia. Congress flees to safety.
October 17: The British under General Burgoyne surrender to General Gates's forces at Saratoga.
December 18: General Washington camps at Valley Forge for the winter.
1778
February 6: The United States forms an alliance with France.
July 11: The French fleet under Admiral d'Estaing arrives off New York.

However, General Washington managed to keep his army intact and gradually turned the tide against Great Britain's professional soldiers. Although the Americans had little experience of organized warfare, most of them were experienced with guns. Thomas Jefferson commented that every soldier in the American army had been "intimate with his gun from his infancy." Also, most of the American troops believed in their cause. They felt that they were fighting for their homes and for freedoms that they valued.

By contrast, the British were 3,000 miles from their home base, and they were fighting in hostile country. In 1776 they began to use German mercenaries, called "Hessians," who eventually made up a third of the British forces and became the focus of American hatred. Benjamin Franklin cursed the British for "bringing foreign

Above: *An artist's impression of the* American Turtle *preparing to attack British warships off Staten Island, New York—the first submarine operation in the history of warfare.*

BUSHNELL'S *TURTLE*

The world's first submarine attack was made by an American vessel, the *American Turtle*, on September 7, 1776. It tried to blow up the HMS *Eagle* in New York Harbor, but failed.

The *Turtle* was designed by David Bushnell, a graduate of Yale University. It was just over seven feet long and made of wood. The operator propelled it underwater by a system of levers and pedals. Bushnell's idea was that the *Turtle* would steal up alongside a warship at anchor and attach a cask of gunpowder to its hull. Then the *Turtle* would slip away before a timing device made the powder cask explode. But, in practice, the *Turtle* was not a success. The fate of the *Turtle* after the war remains a mystery.

JOHN PAUL JONES (1747–1792)

The American colonies were rich in shipowners and sailors. In October 1775 they set up their own navy. A Scottish-born captain, John Paul Jones, proved himself the star of the rebels at sea. He raided British vessels and attacked British ports. In 1779, sailing on the *Bonhomme Richard*, he won a famous victory over two British vessels, the *Serapis* and the *Countess of Scarborough*, off the east coast of England.

Above: *John Paul Jones's ship* Bonhomme Richard *defeats two British vessels in 1779.*

mercenaries to deluge our settlements with blood." However, in reality, the British very rarely used terror tactics against American civilians.

Victory at Saratoga

For a long time, the fighting was indecisive, although generally the British got the better of it. In the winter of 1776–77, Washington scored victories amid the ice and snow at Trenton and Princeton in New Jersey. But General Howe's forces returned to the attack the following summer. In September, Howe defeated Washington at the Battle of Brandywine. Howe's army occupied the rebel capital of Philadelphia, forcing Congress to flee to safety in Baltimore.

Left: *Hessian soldiers, who were hired by the British, on a night patrol. The Hessians had a reputation for cruelty toward both civilians and enemy soldiers.*

Meanwhile, another British army under General John Burgoyne pushed south from Canada. Burgoyne was not a talented general. It was said that during the campaign "he spent half his nights in singing and drinking, and diverting himself with his mistress, who was as fond of champagne as himself." The progress of his army was slow, and, meanwhile, the Americans assembled a larger force to face him. Local farmers flocked to volunteer to fight the invaders. They were joined by Virginia riflemen, known to be skilled sharpshooters.

On September 19, 1777, Americans led by Benedict Arnold stopped Burgoyne's advance in a fierce battle at Bemis Heights, New York. According to Captain Wakefield of the New Hampshire Regiment, "Nothing could exceed the bravery of Arnold...he seemed inspired with the fury of a demon." [11] The British were savaged—in one regiment, only 60 out of 400 men were not hurt. Many of the dead lay unburied, and wolves roamed the battlefield through the nights that followed, feasting on the corpses. The British held their ground until October 7, when they were defeated in another brutal encounter.

Burgoyne then retreated to an exposed encampment at Saratoga. Encircled by American forces, the exhausted British were destroyed by cannon fire and by the sniping of the Virginia sharpshooters. On October 17, Burgoyne surrendered.

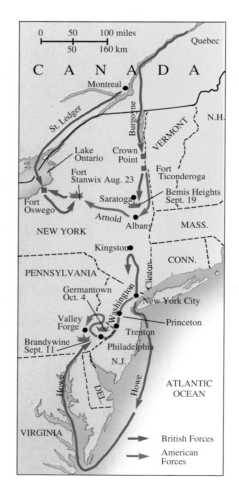

Above: *The red-coated General Burgoyne surrenders to his American opponent, General Horatio Gates, at Saratoga in October 1777. The humiliating defeat of a British army made the world realize that the Americans were capable of winning the war.*

Left: *This map shows the movements of the war in 1777. The British were successful in Philadelphia but the American rebels won an important victory at Saratoga. Note that Vermont was not yet a state, but in 1777 it declared itself an independent territory.*

UNDER FIRE AT SARATOGA

Baroness von Riedesel was the wife of the commander of the Hessian troops at Saratoga. During the rebels' "frightful cannonade," she hid with her children in the cellar of a house. Wounded British and Germans were being treated upstairs. The baroness described what happened: "Eleven cannonballs went through the house, and we could plainly hear them rolling over our heads. One poor soldier, whose leg they were about to amputate, having been laid upon a table for this purpose, had the other leg taken off by another cannonball, in the very middle of the operation. His comrades all ran off, and when they again came back they found him in one corner of the room, where he had rolled in anguish, barely breathing.... In this horrible situation we remained six days." [12]

NATIVE AMERICANS IN THE WAR

The British used Native Americans as allies against the rebels. The Native Americans were fierce warriors and they hated the white settlers, many of whom were trying to steal their land. Urged on by the British, the Cherokees in the south and the Iroquois people, such as the Mohawks and Senecas in the north, joined the war.

Attempts to make the Native Americans fight alongside British troops in battle were not successful. They disliked the British style of warfare. Before a pitched battle with a strong rebel force, the Native Americans just disappeared. They preferred to attack in raids and ambushes.

In 1778 a combined force of four hundred American loyalists led by Colonel John Butler and five hundred Native Americans led by Mohawk chief Joseph Brant raided the Wyoming Valley in northeastern Pennsylvania. Farms and townships were burned and hundreds of settlers were scalped. A British army doctor, John Hayes, claimed that the Wyoming Massacre had "done more to put an end to this rebellion...than all our armies during the war."

But the Native Americans did not have a major effect on the war. The American rebels counterattacked brutally. General Washington ordered the Iroquois country to be "not merely overrun but destroyed." Thousands of Native Americans died in the war and gained nothing from the fighting.

Right: Joseph Brant wearing Mohawk dress.

Joseph Brant (1742–1807)

Joseph Brant, known to Native Americans as Thayendanegea, was a leader of the Mohawk people. As a young man he was taught English and developed close links with British agents. In 1776 Brant visited England and was received at the king's court. During the War of Independence, Brant's Mohawks and Senecas joined in loyalist raids against the rebels. Brant was an intelligent man and a skillful warrior. He was described as "sober, quiet, and good-natured." Brant remained loyal to the British until his death in 1807.

A Hard Winter

Defeat at Saratoga was a great humiliation for the British. Many people had doubted whether the inexperienced American forces could beat the battle-hardened professionals of the British army. Saratoga convinced them that the Americans had a chance of winning.

But victory was still a long way off. During the winter of 1777–78, Washington's army encamped at Valley Forge, 20 miles from British-occupied Philadelphia. The American force was in a wretched condition. One officer, Johann DeKalb, wrote on Christmas Day: "The men have had neither meat nor bread for four days, and our horses are often left without fodder."[13] The weather was bitterly cold, and many of the men only had ragged clothing and no boots.

Below: George Washington and his friend the Marquis de Lafayette walk among the soldiers in the army's winter encampment at Valley Forge, near Philadelphia. Cold and hunger threatened to destroy the Continental Army, but Washington's willpower and determination held the force together.

There were plots to have General Washington dismissed. But he held firm. He appointed a German soldier of fortune, the Baron von Steuben, as inspector general of the army. Von Steuben brought a new discipline and drill to the naturally free-spirited Americans. A young French volunteer, the Marquis de Lafayette, provided Washington with friendship and moral support.

France Joins the War

Since 1775 the American rebels had been receiving secret arms supplies from France. France, controlled by powerful monarchs, was not a democracy and was totally opposed to the principles of freedom and human rights. But France dearly wanted a victory over Great Britain. In 1776 Congress sent Benjamin Franklin to Paris to help negotiate an alliance. The French hesitated, until the American victory at Saratoga showed them that a defeat of Great Britain was possible. In February 1778 a formal treaty was signed committing France to war.

France's entry into the conflict was a turning point. The news was greeted in Washington's camp with shouts of "Long live the King of France!" The British immediately began to withdraw from Philadelphia to New York. They no longer felt secure because the French navy could challenge British control of the sea. In July 1778 the French fleet arrived off New York.

Above: *The Baron von Steuben was a German soldier who volunteered to help the American cause. As inspector general of the Continental Army, he taught the Americans discipline and drill.*

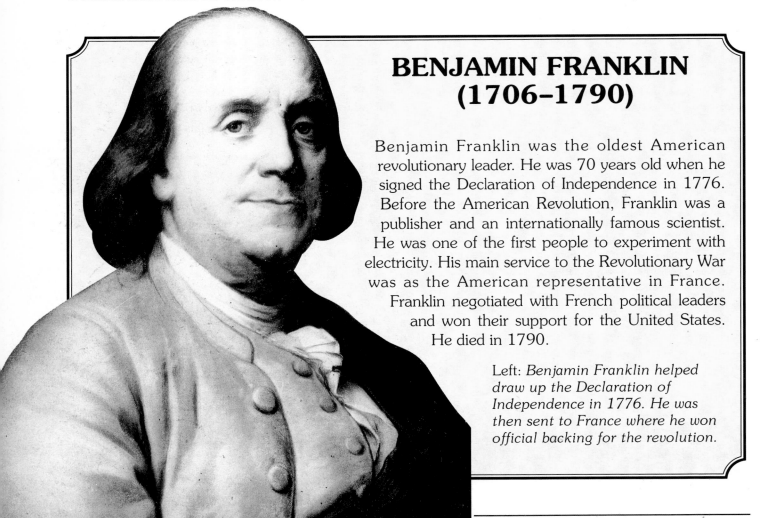

BENJAMIN FRANKLIN (1706–1790)

Benjamin Franklin was the oldest American revolutionary leader. He was 70 years old when he signed the Declaration of Independence in 1776. Before the American Revolution, Franklin was a publisher and an internationally famous scientist. He was one of the first people to experiment with electricity. His main service to the Revolutionary War was as the American representative in France. Franklin negotiated with French political leaders and won their support for the United States. He died in 1790.

Left: *Benjamin Franklin helped draw up the Declaration of Independence in 1776. He was then sent to France where he won official backing for the revolution.*

THE MARQUIS DE LAFAYETTE (1757–1834)

The Marquis de Lafayette was one of the most romantic figures in the American Revolution. He was the son of a rich French aristocrat. When Lafayette was two years old, his father was killed fighting the British. In 1777 Lafayette offered to fight for the Americans. Impressed by his enthusiasm, they made the 19-year-old French youth a major general. Lafayette became a friend of George Washington and fought bravely for the American cause. After returning to France, he supported the French Revolution of 1789.

Below: *General Washington and the Marquis de Lafayette (on the left) shake hands on first meeting in August 1777. Washington was 25 years older than the French aristocrat and developed a fatherly relationship with him.*

THE WORLD TURNED UPSIDE DOWN

Even after the French entered the conflict, the outcome of the war in America was not certain. Washington himself considered it a miracle that the Continental Army was even kept in existence. Feeding and paying the troops presented severe problems. By 1781 the continental dollar, the paper currency issued by Congress, was worth so little that it was used to light fires. The phrase "not worth a continental" entered the language. Militiamen and soldiers mutinied for lack of pay.

Washington felt the spirit of the revolution had become hopelessly corrupted. "Speculation…and an insatiable thirst for riches seem to have got the better of almost every order of men," he wrote. "Virtue and patriotism are almost extinct."[14] Yet by the end of 1781, the British were totally defeated.

Above: General Sir Henry Clinton was commander in chief of the British forces in America from 1778 to 1782.

Below: *The British captured the rich port of Charleston, South Carolina, in May 1780. Here, the British attack the town from land and sea.*

The War Moves South

Until the winter of 1778, all the major fighting had taken place in the northern states. But then the British government decided that their army should now strike in the south. At first this brought major victories. Under General Clinton, who had replaced General Howe as commander in chief, the British quickly captured the prosperous ports of Charleston in South Carolina and Savannah in Georgia. An American force led by General Horatio Gates, the victor of Saratoga, was destroyed by General Charles Cornwallis's troops at Camden, South Carolina, in August 1780.

SLAVES

Black slaves made up one-fifth of the American population. In the northern United States, most people were opposed to slavery. Many slaves and free African Americans fought alongside whites in the Continental Army. But most slaves lived in the southern states. Southern whites feared that the British would encourage the slaves to rise against their rebel owners. James Madison, a Virginian and future president, wrote in 1774: "I am afraid an insurrection among the slaves may and will be promoted." [15]

A slave at work on a small farm in the southern United States. Slaves longed for freedom from their masters, who bought and sold them like animals.

The British were reluctant to call on slaves to revolt. This was partly because Great Britain sought the support of white loyalists in the southern states. These loyalists, like the rebels, were mostly slave owners. But the British did encourage slaves to desert rebel masters, promising them their freedom at the end of the war. However, slaves who deserted loyalist masters were sent back to their owners.

Britain very rarely used slaves in battle. Some southern slaves did get hold of weapons, however, and fought as loyalists in the Savannah swamps. Calling themselves The King of England's Soldiers, they went on fighting for their freedom even after the Revolutionary War had ended.

TIME LINE

1778
August 29: A joint French and American assault on Newport, Rhode Island, fails.
December 29: The British capture the port of Savannah, Georgia.
June 21: Spain declares war on Great Britain.
1780
May 12: The British under General Sir Henry Clinton capture Charleston, South Carolina.
July 11: The Comte de Rochambeau's French force arrives off Rhode Island.
September 25: The traitor Benedict Arnold flees to the British.
1781
January 17: Daniel Morgan's American forces defeat the British at Cowpens.
October 19: General Cornwallis surrenders at Yorktown, effectively ending the War of Independence.

Above: *Nathanael Greene, the commander of the Army of the South, was one of the most successful American generals in the War of Independence.*

Southern loyalist regiments fought alongside the British. But the South Carolina militia led a strong rebel resistance to the British occupation. Their two most famous commanders were Thomas Sumter, known as the Carolina Gamecock, and Francis Marion, the Swamp Fox. Using guerrilla tactics, they terrorized local loyalists and weakened the British forces.

The war became brutal and pitiless as rival regiments of loyalists and rebels rampaged about the country, burning and pillaging as they went. The Southern Department of Washington's Continental Army, commanded by the brilliant General Nathanael Greene, also fought a virtual guerrilla war. With only two thousand men, mostly ill-equipped and half-starved, Greene harassed the British. He said: "We rise, get beat, rise, and fight again." [16]

While rebel guerrilla attacks drove the British out of most of South Carolina and Georgia, General Cornwallis boldly struck northward through North Carolina into Virginia. His forces suffered heavy losses in some bloody fighting. At Kings Mountain, one thousand Tennessee loyalists were surrounded by tough frontiersmen and massacred. At Cowpens, on January 17, 1781, the British lost nine hundred men, while the Americans lost just seventy-two. On August 1, 1781, Cornwallis's disastrous march ended at the small port of Yorktown on the shore of Chesapeake Bay, Virginia.

SIR BANASTRE TARLETON (1754–1833)

The son of a merchant in Liverpool, England, Captain Tarleton was the commander of the British Legion, a force that terrorized rebels in the south. Only twenty-six years old in 1780, he boasted that he had "butchered more men...than anyone else in the army." Tarleton was a dashing young cavalry officer, famous for driving his horses to the limit and using speed and surprise to overwhelm his enemies. But he was also noted for the cruel killing of defenseless prisoners. He lived to a ripe old age.

Right: *British Major John André appears casual and relaxed as American soldiers arrive to take him to the gallows. Even many American officers thought the execution of André for spying was wrong.*

TREASON!

In the early years of the War of Independence, Benedict Arnold was one of the most successful American generals. But he felt that Congress did not sufficiently reward him for the efforts he had made at Saratoga. Heavily in debt, he decided to sell his services to the British.

In September 1780 Arnold secretly met British Adjutant General Major John André to arrange this betrayal. Arnold was to let the British capture West Point, the fortress he commanded on the Hudson River, in return for £20,000. But André was taken prisoner by rebel militiamen as he returned to the British lines, and the plot collapsed.

Arnold fled to the British, who gave him money and made him a brigadier general in their army. André, on the other hand, was tried by the rebels and condemned to be hanged as a spy. He went to his death with great dignity, addressing those present: "I pray you, to bear me witness that I meet my fate like a brave man." Then, watching the noose being prepared, he murmured: "It will be but a momentary pang." [17] These were his last words.

Surrender at Yorktown

A French force of 5,500 men under the Comte de Rochambeau had arrived in America in July 1780. Up to this point, French intervention in the war had not had a dramatic effect. Now it was to prove decisive. In September 1781, learning that Cornwallis was in Yorktown, Washington planned a bold land-sea operation to trap him there. A French fleet, under Admiral François-Joseph-Paul de Grasse, would sail from the West Indies to blockade Chesapeake Bay. At the same time, Washington and Rochambeau would hurry south to cut off Cornwallis from escape by land.

The plan worked. Admiral de Grasse drove off a Royal Navy attack and blocked the bay. Washington and Rochambeau met at Williamsburg, Virginia, on September 28. Their combined force of almost 17,000 men laid siege to Cornwallis's 8,000 soldiers in Yorktown. The British had no defense against the French and American cannons, which rained down fire on their positions. Bodies lay unburied in the streets with heads and limbs shot off. Cornwallis's headquarters were hit, and he had to move

Above: *The French fleet prevented the Royal Navy from coming to the aid of the British army at Yorktown.*

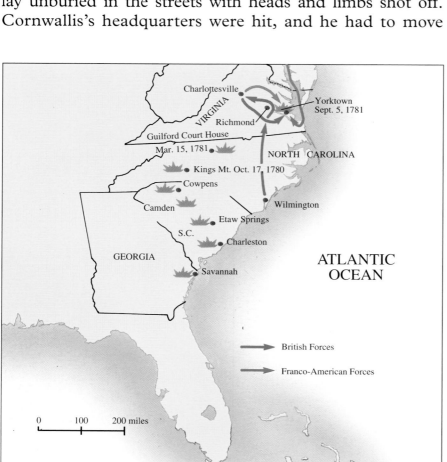

Left: *This map shows the main battles from 1778 to 1781.*

into a cave. People hid in improvised shelters by the shore, but these offered little protection. Food supplies were soon almost exhausted, and soldiers deserted in droves.

On October 17, a British officer walked toward the Americans waving a white flag and asked for terms for surrender. Two days later, the British soldiers in their bright scarlet uniforms marched out of Yorktown and piled their arms in front of the victorious French and Americans. Some wept and some swore. While they performed this melancholy ceremony, the British troops played an appropriate old tune, "The World Turned Upside Down."

Below: *The British redcoats march out to lay down their weapons after the surrender at Yorktown.*

THE BIRTH OF A NATION

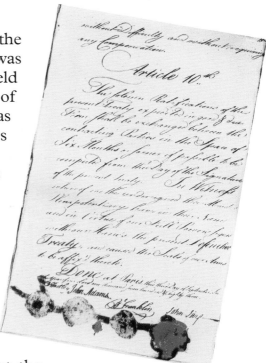

After the surrender of Cornwallis at Yorktown, the British gave up trying to win the war. There was no more serious fighting, and peace talks were held in Paris. On September 3, 1783, in the Treaty of Paris, Great Britain recognized the United States as an independent country. The last British troops withdrew from New York on November 25.

About 100,000 loyalists left the United States either during or after the revolution. Many of those who emigrated had been powerful landowners or merchants. Many other members of the rich elite had supported the revolution. These essentially conservative men remained in control of the United States after the British left. They did not want a social upheaval. They wanted to keep life very much unchanged. Their main concern was to arrange politics in the new United States so that the abuses that had caused the revolution could never happen again. They wanted to guarantee that the government would never be able to take away the basic freedoms they had fought for.

The Path to the Constitution

During the War of Independence, Americans had begun to develop a sense of national identity for the first time. But the states remained essentially independent. Each state raised its own revenue and voted its own constitution.

In 1781 the 13 states were formally joined together under a single central government by the Articles of Confederation. But the central government was very weak, and the thirteen state governments still mostly ran their own affairs. People soon began to find this loose confederation unsatisfactory. In 1786 farmers in Massachusetts, led by Daniel Shays, rebelled against the state government. Congress was unable to organize effective support for Massachusetts, and the state was only just able to put down the uprising. Many people concluded that a stronger central government was needed to make the United States stable.

In May 1787 a convention met in Philadelphia to draw up a constitution for the United States. Members of the Constitutional Convention included Benjamin Franklin and future presidents George Washington and James Madison. The convention worked to find a compromise between the power of federal government and the power of the state governments. Those present also sought to balance the need for a firm authority to maintain order and the need to guarantee freedom for the individual.

Some people wanted a strong president—like a king—while others wanted Congress to run the country. Then there were bitter arguments among the small states, who wanted all states represented equally in Congress, and the larger states who wanted states to have more or fewer seats in proportion to their population. The southern states were worried that they would not have enough representatives because so many of their people were slaves who had no vote.

Left: This document is the Treaty of Paris, signed in September 1783. In the treaty, Great Britain recognized the independence of the United States. The signatures at the bottom include those of John Adams and Benjamin Franklin.

Below: The victorious American Continental Army marches in to take over New York from the British on November 25, 1783. Although the war had really been won in 1781, it took two years to arrange for the last British troops to leave.

THE QUESTION OF SLAVERY

It was obvious to many Americans that the principles of freedom and equality proclaimed in the Declaration of Independence were a farce, as long as 500,000 slaves remained in bondage in the new United States without any rights or freedom at all. In Massachusetts some black slaves, including Quok Walker and Bett Freeman, took the issue to court in 1781. The court agreed that freedom and equality applied to them, too. This effectively ended slavery in Massachusetts.

Throughout the northern states, the slave trade and then slavery itself were gradually abolished after independence, although there were still slaves in New York State until 1817. In the southern states, where most slaves lived, slavery was not only retained but continued to expand. It was not abolished until 1863.

On September 17, 1787, the Convention agreed a draft constitution, although it was not ratified by all the states until 1790. In April 1789, George Washington, the hero of the War of Independence, became the first president of the newly independent country. The Constitution was a successful compromise between conflicting views and interests. The federal government was strong, but state governments kept some real powers. There was an elected president as head of state, but a system of checks and balances prevented him from having too much power. Congress was divided into two houses: the Senate, which gave all states equal representation, and the House of Representatives, in which states had seats in proportion to their population. To satisfy the southern states, each slave was counted as three-fifths of a person in calculating the number of seats.

Above: *The original document of the United States Constitution. The United States was the first country in the world to be governed according to a detailed written set of rules.*

A Democratic Revolution

The Constitution begins with the words: "We the People..." This was arguably the most important phrase in the whole document. It meant that the government and its institutions existed only by the will of the people. This was the principle that Americans had learned from the revolutionary struggle. Government existed to do what the people wanted, not to

Right: *George Washington (with his hand on the book) is sworn in as the first president of the United States. On his left is the first vice president, John Adams. Washington's dignity and honesty won the presidency great respect.*

THE BILL OF RIGHTS

In 1789 Congress adopted ten amendments to the Constitution. These amendments were known as the Bill of Rights. They were designed to protect the freedom of the individual against the government. They guaranteed Americans freedom of speech, freedom to worship the religion of their choice, and freedom of the press.

The Bill of Rights also stated "A well-regulated militia, being necessary to the security of a free state, the right of the people to keep and bear arms, shall not be infringed." Local militias were vital to the American victory in the War of Independence and were considered important to prevent oppressive government. The right to own a weapon is still upheld as a fundamental freedom by many American citizens today.

AN EXAMPLE TO THE WORLD

The American Revolution created a new model for the world to follow. The United States was the first major country in modern times to be a republic, with an elected president rather than a king or queen. It was also more democratic than any other society of its time. When the countries in South and Central America became independent in the 19th century, they adopted constitutions on the American model. More or less democratic republics have eventually become the most common form of government throughout the world.

Abroad, the influence of the American rebellion was felt most strongly in France. The cost of their contribution to the American war bankrupted the French monarchy, and this led directly to the French Revolution of 1789. The French revolutionaries produced a Declaration of the Rights of Man, modeled closely on the principles of the American Revolution. They also founded a democratic republic. The French Revolution eventually followed a very different course from the revolution in America, through the Reign of Terror to the rule of Emperor Napoleon. But, without the example of the American Revolution, the French Revolution might never have happened.

make the people do what they did not want. This simple phrase introduced the era of democracy.

Of course, the United States was at first a very imperfect democracy. Women, Native Americans, the poor, and African Americans had no vote. Over the years, the system of government would go through many ups and downs. But the democratic principle that the United States had established at its foundation was destined to shape the political future of the world.

GLOSSARY

Allies Allies are on the same side in a war or battle.

Artisans Skilled workers who make goods such as shoes or furniture. Traditionally they work in small workshops and make things by hand, using their own tools.

Boycott To engage in an organized refusal to use a product or service, usually to show disapproval or force acceptance of certain conditions.

Conscript Someone who is recruited or drafted into the army by law or by force.

Constitution A set of rules saying how a society is to be governed. A constitution limits the power of the government and gives citizens rights that they can uphold in court.

Customs duties Taxes imposed on goods entering or leaving a country.

Democratic A system of government in which the rulers are elected by the people whom they rule.

Gavel A small wooden hammer used at auctions and meetings.

Guerrilla tactics Methods used by small forces to try to beat larger ones by harassing them and avoiding major battles. It has been called "the war of the flea," because guerrillas wear down their bigger opponents with hundreds of small bites.

Legislature A body or organization with the power to make laws.

Loyalists Americans who remained loyal to the British King George III and opposed the revolution.

Mercenaries Soldiers who fight for any cause in exchange for money.

Militias Bodies of part-time soldiers rather than professional army fighters. Militiamen usually fight only in their local area and continue with their normal jobs when they are not called upon to fight.

Minutemen American civilians who supported the rebels and, when called upon to fight, could be ready in a minute.

Parliament The supreme legislative body of Great Britain, roughly similar to the United States Congress.

Patriots Americans who supported the rebellion against British rule.

Plantation A large estate, normally worked by slaves, where crops such as cotton or tobacco were produced.

Radicals A general term for people who want a fundamental change in politics or society, rather than minor reforms.

Redcoats The British soldiers were known as "redcoats" because of the scarlet uniforms they wore. The Americans also called them "lobsterbacks."

Republic A country governed by a president or a prime minister instead of a king or emperor.

Sharpshooters American marksmen who could shoot very accurately, usually while hidden from their opponents.

Tarred and feathered A way of punishing someone by public humiliation. The victim was stripped, smeared with tar, covered in feathers, and then paraded through the streets.

Tories Loyalist Americans who disliked the patriots and wanted the colonies to stay under British authority.

FURTHER INFORMATION

BOOKS

Colonial America. A four-book series published in 1993 by Franklin Watts (New York).

Howarth, Sarah. *Colonial People.* People and Places. Brookfield, CT: Millbrook Press, 1994.

Marrin, Albert. *The War for Independence: The Story of the American Revolution.* New York: Atheneum Children's Books, 1988.

Meltzer, Milton. *George Washington and the Birth of Our Nation.* New York: Franklin Watts, 1986.

Meltzer, Milton. *Thomas Jefferson: The Revolutionary Aristocrat.* New York: Franklin Watts, 1991.

Nardo, Don. *Braving the New World: From the Arrival of the Enslaved Africans to the American Revolution (1619–1784).* Milestones in Black American History. New York: Chelsea House, 1994.

Silverman, Jerry. *Songs and Stories from the American Revolution.* Brookfield, CT: Millbrook Press, 1994.

Sourcebook on Colonial America. A six-book series published in 1991 by Millbrook Press (Brookfield, CT).

For older readers

Black, Jeremy. *War for America: The Fight for Independence.* New York: St. Martin's Press, 1991.

Chronicle of America. Harlow, UK: Longman Group.

Cumming, William P. and Rankin, Hugh F. *The Fate of a Nation.* London: Phaidon Press, 1975.

Hibbert, Christopher. *Redcoats and Rebels: The American Revolution through British Eyes.* New York: W. W. Norton & Co., 1990.

Fiction

Collier, James and Collier, Christopher. *My Brother Sam Is Dead.* New York: Scholastic, 1985.

Cooper, James Fenimore. *The Last of the Mohicans.* New York: Penguin Books.

Forbes, Esther. *Johnny Tremain.* Houghton Mifflin, 1943. Available from Dell Yearling Books (New York).

Poems

"The Concord Hymn" by Ralph Waldo Emerson
"Paul Revere's Ride" by Henry Wadsworth Longfellow

FILMS

Johnny Tremain (1957)
The Last of the Mohicans (filmed in 1936, 1977, and 1992)
The Rebels (1979)
Revolution (1985)
1776 (1972)

SOURCES OF QUOTES

1   Quoted by Jeremy Black in *War for America* (St. Martin's Press, 1991).
2   Quoted by R. B. Nye and J. E. Morpurgo in *The Birth of the USA* (London: Penguin, 1967).
3   Quoted in *The Correspondence of King George III with Lord North, 1768–1783* (New York: Oxford University Press, 1971).
4   Quoted by Jeremy Black in *War.*
5   Quoted in *Chronicle of America* (Longman).
6   Quoted by Christopher Hibbert in *Redcoats and Rebels* (W. W. Norton, 1990).
7   Quoted by William P. Cumming and Hugh F. Rankin in *The Fate of a Nation* (Phaidon, 1975).
8   Quoted by Christopher Hibbert in *Redcoats.*
9   As above.
10 Quoted in *The Blackwell Encyclopedia of the American Revolution* (ed. Jack P. Greene and J. R. Pole. Oxford: Blackwell, 1991).
11 Quoted by Christopher Hibbert in *Redcoats.*
12 Quoted in *Baroness von Riedesel: Letters and Memoirs Relating to the American War of Independence* (published in New York, 1867).
13 Quoted by William P. Cumming and Hugh F. Rankin in *Fate.*
14 Quoted by James T. Flexner in *Washington: The Indispensable Man* (Boston: Little, Brown & Co., 1974).
15 Quoted by Jeremy Black in *War.*
16 Quoted in *The Blackwell Encyclopedia of the American Revolution.*
17 Quoted by Willard Sterne Randall in *Benedict Arnold* (London: Bodley Head, 1991).
18 Quoted by Cristopher Hibbert in *Redcoats.*

INDEX